Read for a Better World™

BASEBALL
A First Look

PERCY LEED

GRL Consultant, Diane Craig, Certified Literacy Specialist

Lerner Publications ◆ Minneapolis

Educator Toolbox

Reading books is a great way for kids to express what they're interested in. Before reading this title, ask the reader these questions:

What do you think this book is about? Look at the cover for clues.

What do you already know about baseball?

What do you want to learn about baseball?

Let's Read Together

Encourage the reader to use the pictures to understand the text.

Point out when the reader successfully sounds out a word.

Praise the reader for recognizing sight words such as *in* and *the*.

TABLE OF CONTENTS

Baseball 4

Baseball

Many kids play
baseball.
They play in spring
and summer.

ball

bat

You need a bat and ball.

You need a glove.

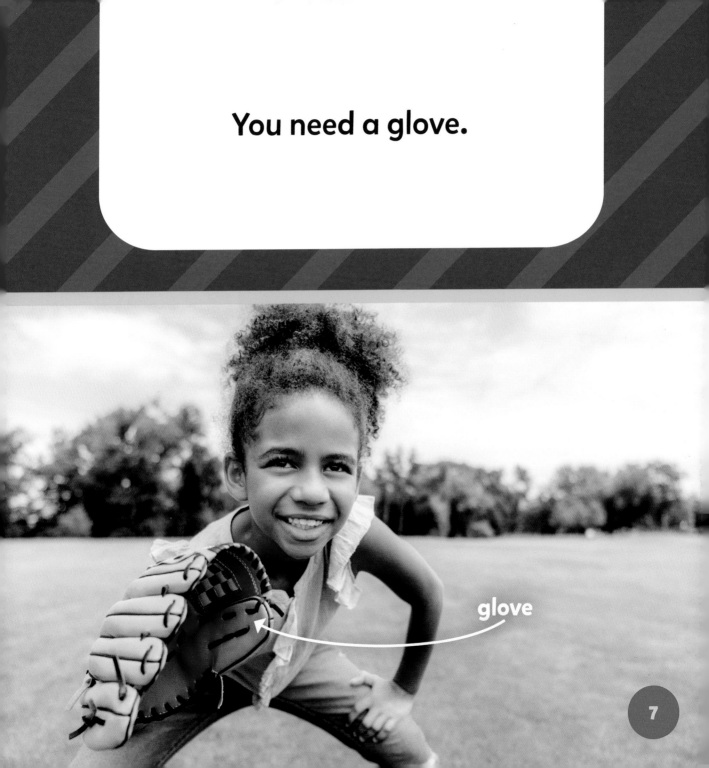

glove

One team starts
in the field.
The other team bats.
They switch after
three outs.

The pitcher
throws the ball.
The batter swings
the bat.

Would you like to
pitch or bat?

The batter may miss.
This is a strike.
A batter is out
after three strikes.

The batter hits
the ball.

Why do batters wear helmets?

Fielders try to get the batter out. They catch the ball. They touch the base before the batter.

Why do fielders
wear gloves?

17

The batter goes around all four bases. This is a run.

The team with more
runs wins.

Players and fans have
fun at the ballpark.

You Connect!

Have you ever played baseball before?

What part of a baseball game seems most fun to you?

How could you get better at playing baseball?

Social and Emotional Snapshot

Student voice is crucial to building reader confidence. Ask the reader:

> What is your favorite part of this book?

> What is something you learned from this book?

> Did this book remind you of any sports you play?

Opportunities for social and emotional learning are everywhere. How can you connect the topic of this book to the SEL competencies below?

> Responsible Decision-Making
> Self-Awareness
> Self-Management

Photo Glossary

base

batter

fielder

pitcher

Learn More

Dittmer, Lori. *Baseball*. Mankato, MN: Creative Education, 2020.

Fishman, Jon M. *Baseball Superstar Aaron Judge*. Minneapolis: Lerner Publications, 2019.

Greenwood, Nancy. *I Can Be a Baseball Player*. New York: Gareth Stevens, 2021.

Index

Photo Acknowledgments

The images in this book are used with the permission of: © RBFried/iStockphoto, pp. 4–5; © Eastfenceimage/Shutterstock Images, p. 6; © LightFieldStudios/iStockphoto, p. 7; © mTaira/Shutterstock Images, pp. 8–9, 10–11, 12–13; © RichVintage/iStockphoto, pp. 10, 23 (pitcher); © dreamnikon/Shutterstock Images, pp. 14–15, 23 (batter); © RonTech2000/iStockphoto, pp. 16–17, 23 (base, fielder); © jondpatton, p. 18; © monkeybusinessimages/iStockphoto, p. 19; © kali9/iStockphoto, p. 20.

Cover Photograph: © Digital Media Pro/Shutterstock Images.

Design Elements: © Mighty Media, Inc.

Lerner Publications Company
An imprint of Lerner Publishing Group, Inc.
241 First Avenue North
Minneapolis, MN 55401 USA

For reading levels and more information, look up this title at www.lernerbooks.com.

Main body text set in Mikado a Medium.
Typeface provided by Hannes von Doehren.

Library of Congress Cataloging-in-Publication Data

Names: Leed, Percy, 1968- author.
Title: Baseball : a first look / Percy Leed.
Description: Minneapolis, MN : Lerner Publications, 2023. | Series: Read about sports (Read for a better world) | Includes bibliographical references and index. | Audience: Ages 5–8 | Audience: Grades K–1 | Summary: "Baseball is a sport enjoyed by all ages. Through engaging, accessible text, young readers learn the basics of this major-league game"– Provided by publisher.
Identifiers: LCCN 2022007937 (print) | LCCN 2022007938 (ebook) | ISBN 9781728475677 (library binding) | ISBN 9781728479002 (paperback) | ISBN 9781728484341 (ebook)
Subjects: LCSH: Baseball—Juvenile literature.
Classification: LCC GV867.5 .L44 2023 (print) | LCC GV867.5 (ebook) | DDC 796.357—dc23/eng/20220224

LC record available at https://lccn.loc.gov/2022007937
LC ebook record available at https://lccn.loc.gov/2022007938

Manufactured in the United States of America
1 – CG – 12/15/22